ATTICIST

EKP

BELLRINGERS

by Daisy Hall

A finalist for the Women's Prize for Playwriting 2023, *Bellringers* was first produced by Atticist and Ellie Keel Productions in a co-production with Hampstead Theatre. It was staged at Paines Plough's Roundabout at the Edinburgh Festival Fringe in August 2024 before transferring to Hampstead Theatre Downstairs from 27 September until 2 November 2024.

BELLRINGERS

by Daisy Hall

CAST

ASPINALL	Paul Adeyefa
CLEMENT	Luke Rollason

CREATIVE TEAM

Director | Jessica Lazar
Designer | Natalie Johnson
Lighting Designer | David Doyle
Sound Designer | Holly Khan
Casting Director | Sarah Jones
Assistant Director | Joseph Winer
Company Stage Manager | Aime Neeme

ATTICIST

Atticist is an award-winning theatre company, aiming to make work that is bold, hopeful, inventive, and exciting. Work that roots around inside our hearts, where the fantastical nightmares lie.

Atticist's first production, *Life According to Saki*, won the Carol Tambor Best of Edinburgh Award at the 2016 Edinburgh Fringe and transferred Off-Broadway in 2017.

Since then, Atticist has produced three acclaimed and award-winning revivals: Steven Berkoff's *East* at King's Head Theatre in 2018, David Greig's *Outlying Islands* at King's Head Theatre in 2019 and a newly-updated version of Lisa D'Amour's *Anna Bella Eema* at Arcola Theatre in 2019. During the pandemic, Atticist commissioned and produced audio drama (in co-production with Ellie Keel Productions, 45North, and North Wall Arts Centre) such as Margaret Perry's *A Passion Play* starring Nicola Coughlan (recorded remotely between Galway, Shropshire, Stratford-upon-Avon, and London), and the interactive *You Play: Vols. 1 and 2* starring Katherine Parkinson and Olivia Williams.

In 2022 Atticist premiered *SAP* by Rafaella Marcus to critical acclaim at Paines Plough's Roundabout, Summerhall, in co-production with Ellie Keel Productions. After a sell-out run, it transferred to Soho Theatre and embarked on a national tour in 2023.

Atticist is run by joint Artistic Directors Jessica Lazar and David Doyle.

EKP

Winner: The Stage Producer of the Year 2024

Founded in 2019, Ellie Keel Productions commissions, develops and produces fearlessly imaginative new plays. Recent work includes the Olivier Award-nominated *The Swell* by Isley Lynn (Orange Tree Theatre, 2023) and *Bullring Techno Makeout Jamz* by Nathan Queeley-Dennis (Roundabout at Summerhall; Royal Court Theatre, both 2023; UK tour, 2024). Other recent productions include the critically-acclaimed and award-winning shows *An Interrogation* by Jamie Armitage (Summerhall, 2023; Hampstead Theatre, 2025), *The Last Show Before We Die* by Mary Higgins and Ell Potter (Roundabout at Summerhall, 2023), *You Bury Me* by Ahlam (Bristol Old Vic, Royal Lyceum Theatre, and Orange Tree Theatre, 2023), and *SAP* by Rafaella Marcus (Roundabout, 2022; Soho Theatre and national tour, 2023). Other notable EKP shows include *Reasons You Should(n't) Love Me* by Amy Trigg (Kiln Theatre, 2021; national tour, 2022), *Collapsible* by Margaret Perry (HighTide Festival at Assembly; Dublin's Abbey Theatre, 2019; Bush Theatre, 2020), *Hotter* by Mary Higgins and Ell Potter (Underbelly, 2019, Soho Theatre and tour), *Still No Idea* by Lisa Hammond and Rachael Spence (Traverse Theatre, Southbank Centre and tour, 2019), and *Fitter* by Mary Higgins and Ell Potter (Soho Theatre, 2019–20).

Hampstead Theatre champions the original, presenting world-class theatre on two ever-transforming stages.

Since its earliest incarnation in a simple hut over 60 years ago, Hampstead Theatre has always attracted outstanding talent, from Harold Pinter, Mike Leigh, and Tom Stoppard to Nina Raine, Roy Williams and Beth Steel – innovators and original thinkers, every one.

As one of London's leading producing theatres, Hampstead Theatre showcases the very best of what's new; taking pride in the premiere of an astonishing debut, an inventive reimagining of an existing work, or an enthralled first-time audience member. It presents plays that are ingenious, surprising and accessible.

Hampstead Theatre's state-of-the-art home is in north west London, offering West End production values – but with tickets at a fraction of the cost. Hampstead believes in thought-provoking stories that are intelligently told, leaving audiences entertained and exhilarated.

hampsteadtheatre.com

The Women's Prize for Playwriting

Founded in 2019 by Ellie Keel and Paines Plough, the Women's Prize for Playwriting 2023 has a simple mission statement: to campaign for equality in the number of male and female writers whose plays are produced on national stages in the UK and Ireland. In 2018, only 26% of new plays on main stages in Britain were by women. In 2022, still only 30% of main stage productions in the UK had a credited female writer – including librettists and adapters.

The Prize's core activity is:

• Running an open call-out for plays by women and non-binary people.

• Selecting the winning script(s) with the help of an experienced reading team and a prestigious judging panel of industry leaders.

• Producing the winning plays on national stages.

• Leading development work on the winning plays and selected scripts on the shortlist.

2020 Winners: Amy Trigg for *Reasons You Shouldn't Love Me* and Ahlam for *You Bury Me*

2021 Winner: Karis Kelly for *Consumed*

2023 Winner: Sarah Grochala for *Intelligence*

Founder Director: Ellie Keel
Founding Partner: Paines Plough
Literary Associate: Tommo Fowler
Communications Assistant: Natasha Ketel

CAST

Paul Adeyefa | Aspinall

Paul Adeyefa is from Stockport in Greater Manchester where he performed at the Plaza Theatre as a youth. He has always had another interest for the natural sciences, and specialised in theoretical physics for his Master's, before finding a way to pursue his passion and begin his professional acting career.

Theatre credits include: *A Midsummer Night's Dream* (Bridge Theatre); *Women Beware Women* (Sam Wanamaker Playhouse); *The Mirror and The Light* (Gielgud Theatre).

Television credits include: *Ransom* (CBS); *A Scottish Soldier* (BBC); and *Good Omens* seasons 1&2 (BBC/Amazon).

Luke Rollason | Clement

Luke Rollason is a performer, writer and clown. He stars as one of the leads in new Disney+ comedy *Extraordinary* produced by Sid Gentle Productions. Luke's performance in *Extraordinary* earned him a place in the Hollywood Reporter's Top 10 TV Performances of 2023. Luke co-wrote and stars in his new BBC Short film *Quiet Life* which is available to watch on BBC iPlayer. Luke performs absurdly creative physical comedy. His first solo show, the one-man nature documentary *Planet Earth III*, performed sell-out runs at the Edinburgh Fringe and at festivals across the country, before being produced by Soho Theatre for two sell-out runs. His most recent solo show, *Bowerbird*, was nominated for the Comedian's Choice Awards at the 2022 Edinburgh Fringe. The show received unanimous four-star reviews from critics including *The List* and the *Telegraph*, who selected it for their best shows of the Festival, calling it 'gloriously daft'. As a comedy writer, he has written for BBC Radio 4, Channel 4's Random Acts, PULPED and LADBible. Other TV appearances include in *Industry* (HBO/BBC) and *Becoming Elizabeth* (Starz). He was nominated for Best Actor at the Maverick Movie Awards for his role in low-budget feature film *Jack*. Luke trained at infamous clown school L'École Philippe Gaulier. He is a member of funk-comedy double act Stepdads, and award-winning physical comedy trio Privates.

CREATIVE TEAM

Daisy Hall | Playwright

Daisy Hall is a writer from Oxfordshire. She was shortlisted for the Women's Prize for Playwriting 2023 and was awarded the Painkiller Prize in 2024. *Bellringers* is her debut play.

Jessica Lazar | Director

Jessica Lazar is a freelance director and part of multi-award-winning theatre company Atticist. She works on new writing, revivals, and adaptations, and is particularly drawn to stories that explore the tension between social facade and human passion. Jessica was an Artist in Residence at Oxford Playhouse in 2019/20 and a Mercury Creative at Mercury Theatre in 2021/22 (where she now coordinates the emerging directors' professional development). Her productions have won the Carol Tambor Best of Edinburgh Award, inaugural SIT-Up Award for 'social impact theatre', Lustrum Award, SoHo Playhouse Medal of Excellence, and been nominated for fourteen Off West End Awards including Best Director and Best Production, as well as the Holden Street Theatre Award and Amnesty International Freedom of Expression Award.

Theatre credits include: Rafaella Marcus's *SAP* (Roundabout @ Summerhall 2022, Vaults 2020) and *The Gift* (Oxford Playhouse 2021); Lisa D'Amour's *Anna Bella Eema* (Arcola 2019); Iman Qureshi's *this is a love story* and Sam Potter's *The Unicorn* (North Wall Arts Centre 2019); David Greig's *Outlying Islands* (King's Head Theatre 2019); Steven Berkoff's *East* (King's Head Theatre, 2018), and Katherine Rundell's *Life According to Saki* (Edinburgh Fringe 2016/New York Theatre Workshop Fourth Street Theatre 2017).

Her style is physically dynamic and creative collaboration sits at the heart of her practice.

Natalie Johnson | Designer

Natalie Johnson is a freelance theatre designer. She was the 2017 recipient of the Liverpool Everyman and Playhouse Prize for Stage Design, and has gone on to design for theatre, musicals, dance and film. In 2023 she was a Creative Associate at London's Jermyn Street Theatre, and the recipient of the Maria Bjornson Design Bursary at the National Theatre.

Theatre includes: *The Good John Proctor* (Jermyn Street Theatre); *Bacon* (SoHo Playhouse NY, UK tour, Finborough Theatre); *John & Jen*, *Dumbledore Is So Gay* (Southwark Playhouse); *Rupture* (West End Women and Girls Centre); *Would You Adam & Eve It* (The John Marley Centre); *Pomona* (The Carne Studio); *SuperHuman* (New Diorama Theatre); *Very Special Guest Star* (Omnibus Theatre); *Flinch* (UK tour); *Catching Comets* (UK tour); *39 & Counting* (Park Theatre); *Macbeth* (Theatre Peckham); *The Rage of Narcissus* (The Pleasance); *The Shadow* (Home MCR); *Tick Tick Boom* (Bridge House Theatre); *Bluebeard* (Alphabetti Theatre); *Twelfth Night* (Bridge House Theatre and Globe Neuss, Germany); *Mydidae*, *Putting It Together*, *The Wasp* (Hope Mill Theatre); *Striking 12* (Union Theatre); *Eris* (The Bunker); *To Anyone Who Listens* (Hen and Chickens); *Othello* (Everyman Theatre).

David Doyle | Lighting Designer

David Doyle is a multi-award-winning lighting designer working across the UK and Ireland as well as internationally. His work has been seen in Ireland, the UK, the Netherlands, France, Czechia, Austria, Kenya, Switzerland, the USA, and Australia. He was nominated for an Offie for Best Lighting Design for *EAST* at the King's Head Theatre.

Recent theatre work includes: *Bullring Techno Makeout Jamz* (Ellie Keel Productions and Royal Court Theatre); *SAP, Anna Bella Eema* (Atticist and Ellie Keel Productions); *Outlying Islands, East* (Atticist); *we were promised honey!, Nation* (YESYESNONO); *Instructions* (Subject Object); *Little Deaths* (Nuthatch and Scissor Kick); *Fabulous Creatures* (Collide Theatre/Arcola Theatre); *Boy in Da Korma* (Jermyn Street Theatre); *The Last Show Before We Die* (Hotter Project), and *ADMIN* (Oisín McKenna).

David also works as a producer and is currently the Executive Producer for Jermyn Street Theatre. He is the joint Artistic Director of Atticist.

Holly Khan | Sound Designer

Holly Khan is a British/Guyanese composer, sound designer and multi-instrumentalist, creating scores for theatre, film and installation.

Most recent theatre work includes: *Our Country's Good* (Lyric Hammersmith); *Sam Wu is not Afraid of Ghosts* (Polka Children's Theatre); *Sylvia* (English Theatre Frankfurt GMBH); *A Child of Science* (Bristol Old Vic); the Olivier-nominated *Blackout Songs, This Much I Know, Biscuits for Breakfast* (Hampstead Theatre); *Tess* (Turtle Key Arts/ Sadler's Wells); *Dreaming and Drowning* (Bush); *I Really Do Think This Will Change Your Life* (Colchester Mercury); *Duck* (Arcola); *Northanger Abbey, Red Speedo* (Orange Tree Theatre); *The Invincibles* (Queen's Theatre Hornchurch); *Unseen Unheard* (Theatre Peckham); *Laughing Boy, Jules and Jim* (Jermyn Street Theatre); *Mansfield Park* (The Watermill); *The Beach House* (Park Theatre); *For A Palestinian* (Bristol Old Vic/Camden People's Theatre) *OFFIE nominated for Best Sound Design* *Amal Meets Alice* (Good Chance Theatre Company, The Story Museum); *Kaleidoscope* (Filskit Theatre Company, Southbank Centre/Oxford Playhouse); *Ticker* (Alphabetti Theatre, Newcastle/Underbelly, Edinburgh/ Theatre503).

Film and installation work includes: *Becoming An Artist: Bhajan Hunjan* (Tate Kids); *One Day* (Blind Summit Theatre, Anne Frank Trust); *Sanctuary* (Limbic Cinema, Stockton Arts Festival); *Song for the Metro* (The Sage Music Centre, Newcastle); *It's About Time* (UN Women/Battersea Arts Centre/Mayor of London); *Their Voices* (RAA & Global Health Film Festival, Barbican).

Joseph Winer | Assistant Director

Joseph Winer's credits as Director include: *I Fucked You in My Spaceship* (Soho Theatre & VAULT Festival – Winner of Origins Award for Outstanding New Work); *Drag Baby* (Pleasance Theatre/King Head's Theatre); *Don't Smoke in Bed* (VAULT Festival); *The Happy Prince* (Watford Palace/Imagine Watford); *9 to 5 The Musical* (City Academy/POSK Theatre) and *Pictland* (Katzpace/Watford Fringe). Assistant Director credits include: *Hamlet* (Iris Theatre) and *Scab* (Arcola). He is an alumnus of Soho Theatre Writers' Lab (Tony Craze Award Longlist) and has directed over thirty productions with young people and community groups.

Aime Neeme | Company Stage Manager

Aime Neeme is an Australian stage manager and theatre maker with a passion for new writing. Past credits include; *Gunter* (Dirty Hare); *Bullring Techno Makeout Jamz, An Interrogation* (Ellie Keel Productions); *Hungry, Black Love, May Queen, Really Big and Really Loud* (Paines Plough); *How to Save the Planet When You're a Young Carer and Broke, Parakeet* (Boundless Theatre).

Sarah Jones | Casting Director

Sarah Jones is a casting director working for theatre and screen. In 2013 she joined the team at The Factory, Barrow Street where she began her casting career with Maureen Hughes Casting. Over the years she moved from Assistant to Associate Casting Director. In 2019, she became Casting Director at the Abbey Theatre. After four years there she started working freelance. Theatre credits include: *Faith Healer, Portia Coughlan, An Octoroon* and *The Weir* (Abbey Theatre); *The Lieutenant of Inishmore* and *The Cripple of Inishmaan* (Gaiety Theatre) and *Once* (Landmark Productions). Screen credits include *Taken Down* and *Rebellion* (RTÉ); *The Winter Lake* (Tailored Films); *Extra Ordinary* (Keeper Pictures).

THANKS

Special Thanks to Inigo Ford, for his calm cooperation; UCH A&E and Paediatrics, for their kindness and skill; Jermyn Street Theatre; Claire at Old Diorama Arts Centre; Nathan Queeley-Dennis; erstwhile bellringer Caroline Lazar for sending us to St John at Hackney, and their Tower Captain Stephen Jakeman for his generosity of time, knowledge, and biscuits; and Tom Ford.

BELLRINGERS

Daisy Hall

Acknowledgements

Enduring thanks to Caolán Murray, first reader of this, and everything.

Fathomless thanks to those indomitable Halls, Eliza, Ian and Julia, for nigh-on three decades of unwavering support, unsolicited grammatical advice, and thievable patterns of speech.

Diolch yn fawr to the long-suffering friends who read this play for, with, and to me: Josie Lovick, Lily Baron, Alex Green and Polly Manning.

Profound thanks to the Royal Court for their support in the development of this play. Particular thanks to Joel Tan, Ellie Horne, Jane Fallowfield, Sam Pritchard, Gurnesha Bola and Ellie Fulcher for all the time and thought they gave to these Bellringers, and for all the encouragement they have given and continue to give me as a writer. Without them this play would be in a drawer, several drafts back, in a parlous state, and I probably still at my desk job, equally parlous.

Marvelling thanks to Alex Lawther and Ragevan Vasan, whose thoughtful, insightful workshopping of this play at a key juncture was absolutely invaluable.

Sonorous thanks to the brave bellringers of St John's at Hackney, particularly to Steve Jakeman for sharing his knowledge with us, and to Becka Rickard, my campanologist-on-call.

Hearty thanks to those generous denizens of London, Megan Williams, Hugh Cross, Chloë Lawrence-Taylor, and Robert Seatter, who are all so good and so kind.

Disbelieving thanks to the Women's Prize for Playwriting and Ellie Keel for their belief in this play, and to Mel Kenyon for her belief in me.

And everlasting thanks to Ann Dingle, who never could manage a whole apple, and in whose garden this play was begun.

D.H.

For my family
Julia, Ian, Eliza, and Ann

Characters

ASPINALL
CLEMENT

Note on Text

/ indicates an interruption

[text in square brackets is not said]

– is an active lack of speech

This text went to press before the end of rehearsals and so may differ slightly from the play as performed.

Sound of heavy rain. A bell tower, during a storm, at night. It is some time in the hazy past – between the twelfth and eighteenth centuries.

There is something organic happening here, with ferns and moss inside the tower. These might be seen to grow, as if the church is being reclaimed by the earth.

There is a door on the left wall which leads to the churchyard, and a door on the back wall which leads to the rest of the church. Two bell ropes hang down in the centre.

Lightning flashes. Six seconds later, thunder rumbles.

Two people burst in through the left door, letting in a lot of rain. They have to force the door shut against the wind.

ASPINALL *lets out a whoop, as in, 'What a storm!'*

CLEMENT *fishes in his jacket pocket for cigarettes.*

ASPINALL *shakes his hair violently, spraying* CLEMENT *with water.*

CLEMENT *has a cigarette in his mouth.*

CLEMENT. Hey!

   ASPINALL *grins.*

   CLEMENT *takes off his jacket. He sits on a bench. He lights up with a modern lighter.*

   ASPINALL *is examining the bell ropes, walking around them.*

ASPINALL. How long do you reckon we've got?

CLEMENT (*shrugging philosophically*). Who can say?

ASPINALL. No, I meant tonight.

CLEMENT. Oh. Dunno, could be hours yet.

ASPINALL. Yeah.

I was just thinking it was quick last time.

CLEMENT. It came from the east last time, over Great Tew. It'll be slower tonight.

ASPINALL *is near the bell ropes*.

Don't touch them.

ASPINALL. No, I won't. I'm just looking.

The storm's a way off though, like you said. And we'll have to, you know –

He mimes ringing the bells.

eventually.

CLEMENT. Yeah, eventually. But let's wait until we *have* to, is my point.

Sit down, we're not going to miss it, are we?

ASPINALL *sits down beside* CLEMENT, *who is staring straight ahead.* ASPINALL *looks at* CLEMENT.

What?

ASPINALL. What?

CLEMENT. You're staring at me.

ASPINALL. How can you tell?

CLEMENT. You're in my peripheral.

ASPINALL. I'm not.

CLEMENT. I have a wide peripheral. It's something I've just discovered about myself. See these eyes? You don't notice it at first but they're less on the front of my face, more to the sides.

ASPINALL (*peering closely*). Hmmm. Yeah, maybe.

CLEMENT. It's almost imperceptible, but it's there. I've measured. Means I can see further around me than most.

ASPINALL. Like a duck.

CLEMENT. What?

ASPINALL. Predators have eyes on the front, like, you know, dogs. Hawks. Prey animals have eyes on the sides, like ducks.

CLEMENT. I've told you, you can't just believe everything your mother says.

ASPINALL. She didn't tell me this. I observed it.

CLEMENT. I'm not like a duck.

ASPINALL. It's good. I'm saying you can see danger coming. I'm saying you're alert.

Like a hare.

CLEMENT. I am somewhat like a hare. In some ways.

There is a flash of lightning. Five seconds (they count silently), then thunder.

There. Miles off.

ASPINALL. Five miles. Must be over… Bledington?

CLEMENT. Nah, it'll come across Wychwood.

ASPINALL. So over Charlbury, now. Or Cornbury. And then it'll come through Chadlington.

They'll be getting nervous in St Nicholas's.

CLEMENT. Roscoe doesn't get nervous.

ASPINALL. It is him then?

CLEMENT. Yeah. Him and his uncle.

ASPINALL. Well that's good, maybe.

CLEMENT. Is it?

ASPINALL. Roscoe knows what he's about. He says he's got it sorted.

CLEMENT. Roscoe says all kinds of things. He says he saw John the Baptist in the core of an apple.

ASPINALL. Yeah, we all saw that. *You* saw it.

CLEMENT. I saw a shape. I didn't see any meaning in it.

Lightning – thunder.

ASPINALL. I still think they're getting worse.

CLEMENT. What are?

ASPINALL. The storms. Listen to that…

Biblical.

CLEMENT. The architecture's getting to you. All the vaulting – it points your mind upwards. That's why they built them this way. Everything feels a bit biblical in here.

(*Gesturing biblically.*) Lo, a door. Lo, a bench.

ASPINALL. Maybe.

CLEMENT. Lo, a jacket.

What makes a storm biblical, anyway?

ASPINALL. Like the one in the Bible.

CLEMENT. There we go then. This is nothing like that. Let me know when God's picked a new Noah. When the animals start pairing up. When you see the ark taking shape in the dry docks, then we'll talk. Anything else is just weather.

ASPINALL. But you must remember before, when we were kids. The storms were smaller then, weren't they? And they didn't come so often.

CLEMENT. I'm not convinced they were smaller. *We* were smaller, maybe that was it.

ASPINALL. Well, that doesn't / [make sense.]

CLEMENT. I mean perspectives change, is my point.

ASPINALL *delves in a bag or pocket for apples.*

They say everyone grabs on to God at the end.

ASPINALL. The end?

CLEMENT. Or the middle. Everyone turns to God in the middle or the end, if they haven't at the start. That's what they say.

What've you got?

ASPINALL. Apples.

CLEMENT. Where'd you get these?

ASPINALL. I found them.

CLEMENT. Found them where?

ASPINALL. On a tree. They were growing in the witch-house garden – but these ones had come right over the wall. They're fair game I reckon, from a legal perspective.

Do you think he'd have minded?

CLEMENT. The witch?

ASPINALL. Well he wasn't a witch, was he? It was just his house that was witchy.

CLEMENT. He doesn't need apples any more. *We* need apples. I didn't know this tree was there – if it had been me, I'd have climbed right over. If things go well tonight, we'll go back there with a bag tomorrow,

You never used to eat so many apples.

ASPINALL. Didn't I?

CLEMENT. No. Now you're never without one.

ASPINALL. I like the way they feel.

CLEMENT. In your hand.

ASPINALL. In my hand. In my pocket. I feel ready when I've got an apple in my pocket.

CLEMENT. Yeah.

ASPINALL. I take apples on walks.

CLEMENT. Like dogs.

ASPINALL. Yeah, imagine. A little apple on a lead. But I eat them halfway through, and that's no way to behave with a dog, is it?

CLEMENT. Well *I* don't think so, no.

ASPINALL. I eat them halfway through, and then I fling the core.

CLEMENT. Fling?

ASPINALL. Yeah.

CLEMENT. Fling it where?

ASPINALL. Wherever. Into the fields. If the corn is ripe and my throw is good, I can get it far out, get it making ripples in the corn like there would be in a pond – gold instead of blue.

CLEMENT. And what fishes would swim under such gold, I wonder?

ASPINALL. I was thinking they'd be related to rabbits, somewhere way back.

CLEMENT. Or dormice.

ASPINALL. Swimming through the corn stems.

CLEMENT. Suspended in some medium as yet undiscovered.

ASPINALL. I imagine them growing into trees.

CLEMENT. Trees?

ASPINALL. The apple cores. Some of them might grow. They'd be a sign that I was there.

CLEMENT. You've been everywhere. There can't be a patch of ground within five miles you haven't trodden at one time or another. In fifty years the whole place will be an orchard.

ASPINALL. I like that. An orchard for the fish.

CLEMENT. And you. You'll be there.

ASPINALL. Yeah.

Or… even if… I mean, we wouldn't *have* to be there. Even if it's just the orchard it's enough, I think.

CLEMENT *stands, paces.*

CLEMENT. I saw a toad today.

ASPINALL. Where?

CLEMENT. Out there, in the graveyard. It's gone now.

ASPINALL. You were out in this?

CLEMENT. No, earlier – before the rain started. You know what I'm like in that bit before. No good to anyone, just glowering around the house. Probably something to do with the pressure dropping. They could use me as a barometer in a pinch. When I begin to glower, batten down the hatches. They sent me out.

ASPINALL. What were you doing in the graveyard?

CLEMENT *(slightly evasive).* Just sitting. There's a bench.

ASPINALL *knows* CLEMENT *is lying.*

And the trees are nice. Yew.

ASPINALL. Me?

CLEMENT. No, yews and willows.

ASPINALL. Ah.

CLEMENT. Old trees. Tall. Means you can't see the fields, which is getting to be a blessing.

You haven't asked about the toad.

ASPINALL. Tell me about the toad.

CLEMENT. It was mourning.

ASPINALL. How d'you know?

CLEMENT. Well, I'm making assumptions, it's true. But it was sitting by a headstone, weeping, so I'm fairly certain it was mourning.

ASPINALL. Whose grave?

CLEMENT. The rat-catcher.

ASPINALL. Mr Thomas?

CLEMENT. No, two, three rat-catchers back. The… tall… dark hair.

ASPINALL. Mr Baron.

CLEMENT. Mr Baron!

ASPINALL. I liked him. Poor Alf. He could *dance*.

CLEMENT. He could dance.

And he made a better fist of the rat-catching than these new ones. Mr Lovick's going about it with knives.

ASPINALL. Knives.

CLEMENT. And I mean, who in their right mind would give him *access* to the big knives I wonder? Certainly no one who ever sang in his choir.

ASPINALL. You'd not have lived through a single evensong.

CLEMENT. Exactly. Now he stalks the rats with a carving knife.

ASPINALL. Like in the song.

CLEMENT. Well, that's his thinking I'm sure, but those were mice, hence why it's not working.

ASPINALL. What do you think it means?

CLEMENT. I think it's just a song.

ASPINALL. No, I mean the toad.

CLEMENT. Means? I think it means he was a friend of the deceased. Or a relative – by marriage, one assumes. Those are the reasons you mourn.

ASPINALL. I'll ask my mum.

CLEMENT. About the…

ASPINALL. About what it means.

CLEMENT. Don't ask your mum.

ASPINALL. Why not?

CLEMENT. Because we know what she'll say.

ASPINALL. Yeah, she'll say

TOGETHER. It's the end of the world.

CLEMENT. It's always the end of the world. Just like when all the dogs jumped in the river.

ASPINALL. She might be right.

CLEMENT. If she is, I don't want to know about it.

Pause.

ASPINALL. Martha /

CLEMENT. How does it help, is my point? Knowing?

Sorry, what about Martha?

ASPINALL. She was supposed to be getting married today.

CLEMENT. Martha your cousin Martha or Martha the librarian?

ASPINALL. Librarian.

CLEMENT. Who's she marrying this time?

ASPINALL. Someone from Hooky.

CLEMENT. Do you we think she's murdering them?

ASPINALL. Stop it.

CLEMENT. Three in a row, fallen down the well. That's suspicious, I'd say. One, fine. Two, that's shocking bad luck. But three?

ASPINALL. We'll keep an eye.

CLEMENT. We'll hope he can swim.

ASPINALL. Still, it would have been nice. I like weddings. I like seeing everyone in a hat. It's been ages since anyone got married.

CLEMENT. Hang on, why didn't I know about this wedding? Why weren't we invited?

ASPINALL. I was invited, actually.

CLEMENT. What? This is an outrage. Why would she invite you and not me?

ASPINALL. Probably because of all those books you stole.

CLEMENT. You can't steal books from a library, they *want* you to take them.

Who else did she invite?

ASPINALL. Roscoe.

CLEMENT. Roscoe? The mad boy of Chadlington and not Clement, of this parish, part of the beating heart of this town since before I could *spell* civic duty?

ASPINALL. People like him. When he's not exploding things. And he's always around here, conducting his experiments.

CLEMENT. She'll have meant me too. In inviting you, she was inviting me, everyone knows we come as a pair.

ASPINALL. Yeah, that'll be it.

CLEMENT. –

Do you know why they grow yew trees in graveyards?

ASPINALL. I heard it was to stop sheep grazing on the graves. Very poisonous to sheep, the yew.

CLEMENT. I heard it was to supply wood for the longbows. In times of war, you know. Vital to our boys at Agincourt, that's what I heard.

Do you know how to make a longbow?

ASPINALL. No.

CLEMENT. No, nor do I. But it can't be that difficult, can it? I mean it's just – (*He sketches in the air with a finger.*) stick, string, arrow – which is just another stick. If you needed to, I reckon you could do it.

ASPINALL. When would we need to?

CLEMENT. Times of war.

ASPINALL. War with who?

CLEMENT. Maybe all the villages will be riven by factionalism. Little Rollright swears fealty at last to Great Rollright. They sign a treaty with Middle Barton. They lay siege.

ASPINALL. And our allies?

CLEMENT. Hook Norton rides to our aid. Chadlington sends arms. But from Kingham, no word.

Pause.

ASPINALL. It would never happen.

CLEMENT. No.

ASPINALL. I've got cousins in Little Rollright – or did have. Friends too. And, wait a second, your dad's *from* Middle Barton, isn't he?

CLEMENT. Yeah. I was just talking.

Just good to be ready for things. That's what I'm saying. Like, later, I was thinking that – Aspinall, I was thinking that /

ASPINALL. The priest!

CLEMENT. What?

ASPINALL. I knew there was something else. Martha's wedding and the priest's funeral, both rained off.

CLEMENT. –

Where've they put him then? The priest?

Not through there?

ASPINALL. No, no. They're keeping him in the schoolhouse. There's a vigil, day and night. If we weren't here, we'd be there, but they took us off the rota, on account of this.

CLEMENT. Lucky us.

ASPINALL. Well, it was our turn. Had to come around again.

CLEMENT. Yeah, quicker and quicker.

Let's hope this breaks soon. Remember the landlord? Five days of solid rain before they could get him in the ground and even then…

CLEMENT *shudders*.

ASPINALL. Who'll do the priest's funeral?

CLEMENT. Who guards the guards?

ASPINALL. Who nurses the nurses?

CLEMENT. Who cooks the cooks?

–

ASPINALL. But really /

CLEMENT. Wait, wait, I'm sure there's another one.

No, never mind.

ASPINALL. Who'll do it?

CLEMENT. Dunno. They aren't lining up any more, are they? I think you could call it scraping the barrel.

ASPINALL. The barrel where we keep the priests.

CLEMENT. Yeah.

ASPINALL. You could do it.

CLEMENT. I could do it. I sometimes think I might find some sense of purpose in the pulpit. I've got an ear for the rhythms of religion, and I've always been a great teller of stories. I could wear a little collar. But they like you to believe in God.

ASPINALL. They're stuck in their ways.

CLEMENT. Yeah.

ASPINALL. Do us a sermon.

CLEMENT. I don't know any sermons.

ASPINALL. You must remember some of it. Who was the last official one? Reverend… Murray. When did he get – (*Points up*.) frazzled?

CLEMENT. Four years ago? Five? He went early.

ASPINALL. You must remember some of what he said.

CLEMENT. I remember the gist, certainly. I remember the
general idea. Love thy neighbour… and a lot about oxen,
I seem to recall. When this is *sheep* country. You've got to
speak to us in a language we understand. I'd be a saint by
now if only he'd explained it all in terms of sheep.

ASPINALL. Go on then.

CLEMENT. What, now?

ASPINALL. Yeah, now.

CLEMENT. Okay. Okay.

CLEMENT *finds a way to look more priest-like. Perhaps he
does something to his hair, or puts a jacket on back-to-front.*

Grab a pew.

ASPINALL *sits down.* CLEMENT *leaps up onto a bench
and raises his arms, ready to orate to* ASPINALL *and the
audience. He intones in a priestly voice.*

The good book tells us that Christ our Lord was born on
earth five times. The first time the word was made flesh, the
flesh that he was made was flaky and white. Yes, dearly
beloved, the first time around God's sergeant on the earth
was a little fish, just like you or me.

ASPINALL. Right, well that's immediately heresy.

CLEMENT. When Jesus came the first time I say unto ye he
was a little fish, and he lived all his life in a pond. He dwelt
among pondweed, and swam in and out of a beam of light,
and died gently at the age of twenty, having grown fat and
old, and his holy flesh was food for the smallest of insects
that lived in that place, and it was good.

ASPINALL. You'll cause a schism.

CLEMENT. And the second time he was a mushroom, born
bursting through the forest floor in Borneo, under the light of

a bright and guiding star and was, soon after, eaten by three wise and vegetarian beasts, who were subsequently blessed with visions of the divine.

And the third time he was a brown bird and he sang songs, presumably hymns, in a field in Wales for three summers, and was much loved by the people that dwelt in that place, who felt themselves lucky – some said blessed – to live in such an Eden.

And the fourth time he was a human and was much remarked upon. And the fifth time, the last time, Christ was born as a little woodlouse, under a dead log. And there are no gospels that tell of what he did.

How's that?

ASPINALL. Well *I* like it. But I don't think they'll let you say it in a church.

CLEMENT. We are in a church.

ASPINALL. In the main part of a church.

CLEMENT. You know who would have been good? As a priest?

ASPINALL. Who?

CLEMENT. Your godmother.

ASPINALL. Oh *yeah*, she would have been great.

CLEMENT. She would have been terrifying.

ASPINALL. Do you feel like she's still here?

CLEMENT. I hope not – it was me that carried her out. If she's snuck back in…

ASPINALL. Thanks for going to get her.

CLEMENT. That's alright. Can't have them piling up in here, can we? I'd struggle to collect my thoughts if we'd just propped her in the corner.

ASPINALL. Was it bad? You can tell me.

CLEMENT. Not one of the worst.

ASPINALL. Not like James?

CLEMENT. No, that was bad. You can still see where it was, that one, look.

ASPINALL. Did she look peaceful?

CLEMENT. Did she look *peaceful*? She'd been struck by lightning, Aspinall.

ASPINALL. Yeah, I know, I just mean... did she look like she was alright with it?

CLEMENT. Yeah. Yeah, pretty peaceful given the circumstances.

What did you mean, 'still here'. Like a ghost?

ASPINALL. You don't believe in ghosts.

CLEMENT. I don't. *You* believe in ghosts.

ASPINALL. I don't. I'm just saying I get a feeling in here.

They said there was a ghost down in Pool Meadow.

CLEMENT. Just some local joker.

ASPINALL. What local joker? The last of the local jokers was Dusty, and he –

CLEMENT. What?

ASPINALL *points upwards*.

ASPINALL. Frazzled. Three storms ago.

CLEMENT. I thought it had been quiet, lately, in the middle of town. It's because he's not there, shouting bile at passers-by.

ASPINALL. You shouldn't talk about him that way.

CLEMENT. Why not?

ASPINALL. He's dead.

CLEMENT. Lots of people are dead.

He was very rude about my hair once. And he pissed in the well.

ASPINALL. Was that true?

CLEMENT. Roscoe said he did.

ASPINALL. 'Roscoe says all kinds of things.' You didn't believe about the apple.

CLEMENT. This one required no leap of faith. He had the face of a man who had just freshly pissed in the well.

ASPINALL. You'll be hoping people don't speak ill of you if we get frazzled.

CLEMENT. They already do speak ill of me.

ASPINALL. You won't be haunting anyone then?

CLEMENT. I might give it a go, I suppose. But more out of curiosity than any real will to revenge.

ASPINALL. He did ring the bell. Dusty. Every time, when it was his turn. He did *do* it.

CLEMENT. Yeah.

ASPINALL. So not all bad, maybe.

CLEMENT. Blessèd be the man who was not all bad, maybe.

A flash of lightning. They count to four. Thunder.

And that's four miles. What's four miles south?

ASPINALL. Chilson? Shorthampton.

CLEMENT. Yeah.

ASPINALL. Do we know anyone in Shorthampton?

CLEMENT. Er… (*Thinking.*) no, not any more.

ASPINALL. What about –

CLEMENT. Fire. Last May.

ASPINALL. But her / husband.

CLEMENT. A hailstone. Big as my head.

ASPINALL. My uncle rang the bells three times.

CLEMENT. Did he?

ASPINALL. Yeah. Got a bit singed the third time, but he came home. He says it's his diet that does it. Handful of oats, every night. And you've got to keep your feet together when you ring, he says.

CLEMENT (*sarcastically*). Well, why didn't you say so before? Simple as that.

ASPINALL. And Billy did it – three times.

CLEMENT. He didn't.

ASPINALL. He did.

CLEMENT. No he didn't, not the third time. He was in the tower, but he didn't touch the rope. Because he was there with his aunt.

ASPINALL. What, she –

CLEMENT. She didn't let him do it. She rang on her own. People do it. Plenty of people do it.

ASPINALL. He didn't tell me.

CLEMENT. No, well.

ASPINALL. I wouldn't have [judged him].

He didn't tell me.

ASPINALL *wanders around the ropes, examining them carefully.*

CLEMENT. Don't touch them.

ASPINALL. I won't.

CLEMENT. –

It just makes sense, mathematically. If you go, and I /

ASPINALL. These are wet again.

CLEMENT. –

Well, they're always going to be, aren't they? Old roof. Thunderstorm.

ASPINALL. Yeah, but you hope, don't you?

CLEMENT. Who fixed this roof, that's what I want to know. Barely worth being inside.

ASPINALL. It was us, wasn't it?

CLEMENT. No, that was *ages* ago. And we did a great job. It's probably been fixed five times since then, they can't pin this on us.

ASPINALL. Do you think they noticed?

CLEMENT. Who?

ASPINALL. All of them.

CLEMENT. That the ropes were wet? Course they did. Look at this – dripping.

ASPINALL. And they knew what it meant?

CLEMENT. Everyone knows what it means.

ASPINALL. And they just went for it anyway.

CLEMENT. Yeah. Like we did, last time.

ASPINALL. Yeah. We didn't even think about not doing it, did we?

CLEMENT. –

No.

ASPINALL. Right, because when there's people you love relying on you, you do whatever, don't you? Whatever you can. Even if the chance is small.

ASPINALL *is looking at the ropes*. CLEMENT *watches him closely*.

CLEMENT. I suppose. I suppose that is the general feeling.

ASPINALL. Roscoe says he's got this new peal that works every time.

CLEMENT. Roscoe says [all kinds of things].

Well that's good. That's great. The storm will come over Chadlington, unless the wind changes /

ASPINALL. which it never does /

CLEMENT. which it never does, and they'll ring their new peal, the storm will be broken up and by the time it gets to us it'll be nothing but wisps of cloud, and the moonlight will crack through over the fields and we'll toddle home and get blissed out on being young and escaping narrowly.

ASPINALL. Yeah. Only, you need five people.

CLEMENT. What?

ASPINALL. For the peal. It's not really a peal with two, is it? And this new one, he says it works every time but you need five people to do it.

CLEMENT. Can't he get five? I know things have been bad over there – but he can get five surely.

ASPINALL. Yeah, yeah. Still five. But five is a lot to gamble.

CLEMENT. Well, yeah. We can't start frazzling people in fives. That would accelerate things by... well, I can't quite work the maths out, but too fast.

ASPINALL. Roscoe says it's not a gamble.

CLEMENT. But he is not a credible man. Except to you, apparently. This is how your leg got broken. A scheme just like this.

ASPINALL. Not *just* like this. He's not asking me to jump off anything this time.

He was still trying to persuade them to give it a go. Maybe he managed it.

CLEMENT. Maybe.

ASPINALL. I was thinking we could go over there next time. You, me, Roscoe, his uncle. And Jegs would do it, I'm sure. We could give it a go – prove it, one way or another. Even if it is a gamble, might be worth a try at this point.

CLEMENT. How's he worked it out? Why's he so sure it'll work, if it's never been tried?

ASPINALL. He's got this science he's developed. I can't
explain it properly – it's all to do with frequencies, and
angels come into it somehow – not the main ones, not like,
Gabriel, but the ones in charge of rain. He's been reading the
apocrypha all year and ringing handbells at small clouds.
He's combining theology, meteorology, and musicology into
a new kind of science. He's going to take it to Oxford when
it's done. Present a paper or something.

CLEMENT. Right.

ASPINALL. You don't think he will?

CLEMENT. I didn't say that. It's just, it's Roscoe. He got your
leg broken.

ASPINALL. Ages ago. We were kids.

CLEMENT. He gets your hopes up.

ASPINALL. I like my hopes to be up.

*Two mushrooms have been growing steadily through the
floor.*

CLEMENT. Look at this! The mushrooms are back again. This
is a disgrace. These weren't here when we got in, were they?

ASPINALL. I'm not sure.

CLEMENT. Well, they weren't. I was asking out of politeness.
I'm very alert.

ASPINALL. Like a hare.

CLEMENT. Like a hare and with the wide peripheral vision of
a hare.

Someone should be studying this. I'm almost certain they
never grew so fast before.

ASPINALL. When we were younger you mean?

CLEMENT. Exactly. When we were younger they grew at
a steady, comprehensible pace, didn't they?

ASPINALL. We comprehended it. Easily.

CLEMENT. We should put some real thought into this, when we get time. Try and work it out. Like, what are the variables? There must have been a change somewhere that's causing this.

ASPINALL. Nothing but changes, these last years.

CLEMENT. Right. So maybe it's the increased rainfall – the floodwater. Or the tremors. Or the ashes from the fires. Or maybe there's something new in the soil.

ASPINALL. Something new in the soil every other day.

CLEMENT. Yeah. Well, not to be callous, but that could well be it, couldn't it? All of them, leaching into the soil. Very nourishing to a mushroom. And suddenly they've found they're able to grow... well, before our very eyes, as the magicians say. That's a good hypothesis, isn't it?

ASPINALL. I'd say so.

CLEMENT. It's perfectly natural for a mushroom to make use of a bounty like that. Who am I to sit in judgement? Let he who is without sin [cast the first stone]. After all, it hurts no one. They're just using what's around them. We have eaten their brethren. They have eaten ours.

ASPINALL. Feels strange though. Makes me think this one could be mostly made of –

CLEMENT. Dusty.

ASPINALL. He'll have heard us talking about him.

CLEMENT. He's probably agreeing with us. He's probably wriggling his gills in embarrassment about the way he used to carry on.

ASPINALL. And then this other one's my godmother.

CLEMENT. Yeah.

She called me slimy once, did I tell you that?

ASPINALL. She was very old. Another generation. That kind of talk was alright when she was young.

CLEMENT. Still, it struck a nerve. Must be an insecurity of mine, I suppose. A buried concern that I am, somewhere near the core, a little slimy.

But she was buried in Heythrop, and only recently. No way has she made it four miles by now, even with plate tectonics and magma and things of that nature. Four miles, and into this mushroom.

ASPINALL. No, the mushrooms do it. Underneath the ground they have roots that stretch for miles, and they're all tangled together, part of this one big thing. These are just the fruit, really.

CLEMENT. They stretch for miles? Four miles?

ASPINALL. Can do.

CLEMENT. All tangled together?

ASPINALL. Yeah. Don't you believe me?

CLEMENT. Of course I do. I just...

I mean, this changes everything.

ASPINALL. What does it change?

CLEMENT. It means these are two heads of the same beast.

ASPINALL. Dusty and my godmother.

CLEMENT. Together at last.

ASPINALL. Come here to pray, maybe.

CLEMENT. Come to ask forgiveness, more like.

Who's slimy now, eh? Doff your caps, ye blasphemers. Don't you know this is a sanctified building?

Another mushroom has been unfurling nearby.

ASPINALL. Clem.

CLEMENT. Ah.

CLEMENT *is alarmed.*

ASPINALL. That's quick, isn't it?

CLEMENT. I'm inclined to agree with you. It's too quick for indoors. And through a flagstone floor? It's much too quick. At this rate the whole church will be a rich stew by Monday.

ASPINALL. We should pick them.

CLEMENT. We should observe them. See what they do.

ASPINALL. What they do is grow,

Maybe the church warden knew how to stop them. Maybe they've only been coming through since she got frazzled.

CLEMENT. When was that?

ASPINALL. January, wasn't it?

CLEMENT. Yeah. I don't think so. It's just like at home. This is a problem our forefathers never had to deal with. Mushrooms in the church. Mushrooms in the school. Mushrooms squeezing their skulls through the kitchen floor. It's a challenge peculiar to our generation, that's what it is.

CLEMENT *touches his own shoulder, unconsciously.*

They get everywhere.

We should work it out properly. Run tests, if we get the chance.

ASPINALL. What kind of tests?

CLEMENT. We'll draw up a table. Measure inches of growth per hour – averages is what we need. Then we can work out if it's getting faster.

ASPINALL. It's definitely getting faster.

CLEMENT. Well, that's our hypothesis but maybe we're wrong. We can prove ourselves wrong this summer – I don't know why we didn't start sooner. We should have been doing *this* the whole time instead of whatever else it is we do.

ASPINALL. I'll add it to the list.

CLEMENT. Yes, add it. At the top, above all that... wait what else is on there?

ASPINALL. We were going to fix the hole in the boat. Take it as far as Port Meadow.

CLEMENT. Oh yeah.

ASPINALL. And we were going to take Eleanor to see the starlings out towards Bicester.

CLEMENT. Yes and she made me promise, in the end, so we had better do it.

ASPINALL. We were going to catch eels in the Evenlode. Although it was John that was going to teach us. That way of doing it with a ball of worms and wool.

CLEMENT. Someone else will know. Someone else will teach us.

ASPINALL. You wanted to train the goat. And you said we'd watch the sun go down from the ridge most days. That'll take time – the best spot's twenty minutes' walk.

CLEMENT. Fifteen. Fifteen if you focus. You *make* it twenty.

ASPINALL. And we were going to learn the constellations – properly, so that when people say *what's that one?* we know – we're really sure, and it's not just you making it up.

And I'm going to teach you to knit a good sock, and you're going to get good enough at chess to beat me one in three.

CLEMENT. One in two.

ASPINALL. One in three was already ambitious.

And then there's all the work to be done. Errands to run. And favours to do, and visiting. And dealing with crises.

CLEMENT. Yes. Okay. And all that's important. But somewhere in there, near the top, put that we need to give serious thought to the mushrooms.

ASPINALL. And why the storms are getting bigger.

CLEMENT. *If* they're getting bigger.

ASPINALL. Which they are.

CLEMENT. If they are, someone should give some serious thought as to why.

ASPINALL. My mum says /

CLEMENT. We know what your mum says.

ASPINALL. And the priest, the real one, before he was frazzled, said it was God's will.

CLEMENT. Yes, well, that is what they say, isn't it? Priests. That's pretty much the main thing they say.

ASPINALL. He said it was a punishment.

CLEMENT. For what, though?

ASPINALL. General sinning.

CLEMENT. That's always been about. There has to have been something specific or how will we ever learn our lesson?

ASPINALL. Maybe someone did something we don't know about. Opened a forbidden jar or something.

CLEMENT. Well, I resent being caught up in the fallout. I've never opened a jar.

ASPINALL. Maybe / it was

CLEMENT. And I don't want to sound ungrateful, but really we just got here, didn't we? In the grand scheme of things?

And I did steal those books, and there was that time I was unkind to my mother, and I never owned up about that window. And probably loads of stuff I don't remember right now. I'd certainly never suggest that I was *good*. Still it rankles to be bearing the brunt like this.

ASPINALL. You are good.

CLEMENT. No, I mean deep down. At my core.

ASPINALL. You are good at the core.

CLEMENT. I think I've got one growing on me.

ASPINALL. What?

CLEMENT. A mushroom. On my back.

ASPINALL. You haven't. I'd have noticed.

CLEMENT. I pick it. I scrub all over. It keeps growing back.

ASPINALL. For how long?

CLEMENT (*shrugging*). A year?

ASPINALL. A *year*? And you never told me? For a whole year?

CLEMENT. I had hoped it might go away. Given time.

ASPINALL. Let's have a look then.

> CLEMENT *shows* ASPINALL *the back of his shoulder.*

Well, you're not wrong. You're growing a mushroom.

It's a miracle! Hey, you're probably in the almanac. Under mushrooms. Brackets, miraculous appearance on the body.

CLEMENT. So you've not got anything like this? It's just me?

ASPINALL. No. Not yet, anyway.

CLEMENT. Are you repulsed?

ASPINALL. Of course not. It's just strange, that's all.

It doesn't mean anything.

CLEMENT. Doesn't it?

ASPINALL. You should have told me. If you've been worrying about it.

CLEMENT. I've hardly been *worrying* about it – when would I find the time? Just a little mushroom, it goes way down the list. Near the bottom, under the fires, the floods, the failed harvests, the mad dogs, the falling masonry, the mutations, the poisonings, the storms /

ASPINALL. Which are getting worse.

CLEMENT. Which appear to be going through a patch of worseness.

–

Maybe if we worked out exactly when it started. The bad patch. When was it, do you think?

ASPINALL. When we were fifteen, things were fine, weren't they?

CLEMENT. Things were fine. We were just pissing about and things were fine – good, even.

ASPINALL. And when we were eighteen?

CLEMENT. Things had started to go awry. D'you reckon?

ASPINALL. Yeah. Something in the air, at least.

I thought that was just getting older, at the time. I took it to be the ebbing-away of innocence.

CLEMENT. Yeah. Me too.

And you know, maybe we were right: things were always this way, it just takes a grown brain to face up to them. Our parents had their own troubles, we know that. We think we're different, but we're just like everyone else, only from the inside.

ASPINALL. Remember when the top field caught fire? When we were kids?

CLEMENT. Of course. Unforgettable, that one. They let us out of school for it. Our first big fire.

ASPINALL. That was an event.

And when the first two-headed lamb was born, that was big news. Just outside Charlbury, wasn't it?

CLEMENT. Yeah, it was Tom's farm. He brought it round.

ASPINALL. And we all turned out to see it, didn't we? A two-headed lamb was unusual then.

CLEMENT. Yeah, that's why they /

ASPINALL. No, no no.

CLEMENT. Sorry.

ASPINALL. I don't like to think of it in the jar.

CLEMENT. I know, sorry.

ASPINALL. But what are we up to now? Five, six heads?

CLEMENT. They say that was a hoax. A trick, that one. Some kids with a needle and thread. They're feral, some of these young ones. They've grown up amongst it.

ASPINALL. Okay, but the fives and fours are real. And they don't go up to Oxford in jars any more.

CLEMENT. No.

ASPINALL. I think seven years ago. Eight, maybe. Things started to get worse. And then this last year...

CLEMENT. We'll look into it. We'll get through tonight and then we'll start taking averages.

ASPINALL. You admit it's getting worse.

CLEMENT. I admit nothing. But I... *concede* that it wouldn't hurt to... try things. Like Roscoe does. Maybe there's something we can do.

ASPINALL. Well, we are doing *something*. We're ringing the bells.

It works. The waves of sound break up the storm. That makes sense, doesn't it? It makes sense to me. Plus the...

He gestures to the churchy surroundings.

We are doing something.

CLEMENT. Of course. Of course we are. I'm just being curmudgeonly. The pressure must have dropped again. Or raised – either way, the needle has swung from glowering to curmudgeonliness.

Lightning. Count to three. Thunder.

ASPINALL. Do you get scared ever? Of the storms?

CLEMENT. Sometimes. The last one brought down an oak on the Saltway like it was nothing. A thousand years old, they said. Gone. They take off rooves. Drown people. It makes sense to be scared.

ASPINALL. Do you get scared of ringing the bells?

CLEMENT. We've practised, haven't we?

ASPINALL. You know what I mean. Aren't you scared of…

CLEMENT. –

No, of course not. We did it last time.

ASPINALL. I was scared last time.

CLEMENT. Yeah, I know – I saw. Your face was getting lit up, again and again. It was so loud, with the storm and the bells.

It went on for ages.

ASPINALL. I thought that might be it.

CLEMENT. Me too.

ASPINALL. And after, when it got quiet, for a second I thought we were dead. And then I thought, 'there's a heaven, and it looks just the same'. That would be funny, wouldn't it?

CLEMENT. It would be disappointing, I'd say. If you got there and it was still raining.

ASPINALL. But you'd know the rain would stop. Up there. That would be the difference.

CLEMENT *paces. He looks at the ropes.*

What are you thinking?

CLEMENT. I'm thinking all kinds of things.

ASPINALL. Do you think we should…

CLEMENT. What?

ASPINALL. I *will* say it – but you need to not be all…

CLEMENT. Well, I'll *try* not to be all...

ASPINALL. I was just thinking maybe we should pray or... something?

CLEMENT. *Pray?*

ASPINALL. Or not *pray*, just /

CLEMENT. I knew it, I *knew* you were getting religious.

ASPINALL. I'm not! I'm just covering all bases – *you* said I should be more pragmatic.

CLEMENT. You've had this far-away glint the last couple of months – a little bit of gold in your eye, like you're gazing out on some sunlit upland.

ASPINALL. I have *not* got a glint.

CLEMENT. I'm sure it's very nice. Very comfortable. I'm up to my waist in floodwater trying to salvage the best pig and you're there glinting, like you've gone somewhere else already.

ASPINALL. I was mourning the pig. That's my mourning face.

CLEMENT. I've seen your mourning face, haven't I? Again and again I've seen it. *This* is different.

ASPINALL. I cry less than you, we don't know why.

CLEMENT *turns away, non-committal.*

(*Grinning.*) I'd give anything for your ability to weep.

CLEMENT. Well, that's foolish.

ASPINALL. I'd like to be able to cry at a sunset. Or at songs.

CLEMENT. It's an affliction, this thing I have these days. With the music.

ASPINALL. It's natural.

CLEMENT. It's natural if the music's particularly rousing or particularly sad. If there are oboes. But now I –

Last week the baker was whistling and I had to ask him to stop.

I mean, I was always one to well up on occasion, it's true. But since last year – well, since Mum was, er…

He points upwards at the bells.

This is uncharted territory.

ASPINALL. *I* think it's natural.

It'll pass. Or, no. I mean… it'll lessen. It's not been long, in the scheme of things. Before, we would have said it had been no time at all. A year would have been nothing, before.

CLEMENT *touches the place on his shoulder where the mushroom is.*

CLEMENT. Do you think this one's her?

ASPINALL. Your mum?

CLEMENT *nods.*

Come to spend time with you?

Could be. I'd like to believe they come back.

CLEMENT. Like ghosts?

ASPINALL. Yeah.

CLEMENT. So would I. I really would like to Aspinall.

Come on then. Let's pray.

ASPINALL. No, no, you're right. I was getting carried away. Vaulted ceilings.

CLEMENT. I mean it. I want to. How do we go about it? Do we kneel?

ASPINALL. Can do. Not strictly necessary, of course.

CLEMENT *kneels.* ASPINALL *follows suit.*

CLEMENT. No. But it's the done thing around here, isn't it?

ASPINALL. Helps to distinguish between praying and just talking I suppose.

They put their hands together and close their eyes.

–

–

CLEMENT. I thought we were doing it out loud.

ASPINALL. We are.

CLEMENT. Well, go on then.

ASPINALL. I thought you were doing it.

CLEMENT. Why?

ASPINALL. I don't know.

CLEMENT. This is your idea. You're the reverent one. I'll just amen at the end and it'll count for both of us.

ASPINALL. Okay.

–

I can't. Not with you watching me.

CLEMENT. I'm not watching you.

ASPINALL. I'm in your peripheral.

CLEMENT. My eyes are closed.

ASPINALL. You have the peripheral of a hare.

CLEMENT. But my *eyes* are *closed*.

ASPINALL. You do it.

CLEMENT. I'm an atheist. I'm indulging you.

ASPINALL. You can make it sound right.

CLEMENT. –

Fine.

O God, who maketh the gathering storm and the little microbe, who raiseth both the tree and the wind that knocks it down,

who said, 'Let there be apples', and there were apples, and
who said, 'Let there be worms', and it was so, hear our prayer.
We tiny mortals, motes of dust on the hem of your
incalculable majesty, we humbly beg your godly protection.

*More mushrooms spring into existence on the walls and
floor.*

ASPINALL *and* CLEMENT *have their eyes shut.*

CLEMENT *touches his shoulder again.*

(*More serious, now.*) We who have, in the scheme of things,
done very little wrong. Nothing that might be considered
cardinal for my part, and nothing at all for his. There's
a rumour going around that you're punishing us or testing us
with a lot of fire and brimstone and floods and fungus. And
locusts, canker sores, and rot, and madness, and high winds,
and desperation. Mutations, bad dreams, loneliness, rage /

ASPINALL. The fish.

CLEMENT. What?

ASPINALL. The rains of fish.

CLEMENT. And the rains of fish, also. And I'd ask you to stop,
but there doesn't seem much use – I don't know if that
counts as more than one wish – prayer, sorry.

But some people say you love bellringers best of all. And if
that's true then we'd only like to live – for ages, ideally. But
at least through the night.

ASPINALL. Amen?

CLEMENT. Amen.

ASPINALL. Amen. That was good.

CLEMENT. A bit off-the-cuff. I could do better. If I had time.

CLEMENT *lies down on a bench.*

I don't know if we really need *delivering* from the rains of
fish. They're a nuisance more than an existential threat for

the most part, Mr Welbourne aside. Sometimes they're quite useful, even. Did you think we'd be eating mackerel, ever, this far from the sea? Or bass?

ASPINALL. They're ominous.

CLEMENT. Pollock.

ASPINALL. I mean they're a bad omen – one of the really official ones.

CLEMENT. Well, yes. Particularly for Mr Welbourne.

ASPINALL. But in general.

CLEMENT. Imagine making it to eighty-four and then – boom – run through with a swordfish. Makes you think, doesn't it?

ASPINALL *is frustrated, in a small way, that* CLEMENT *is not listening to him.*

CLEMENT *realises* ASPINALL *is annoyed. He sits up.*

And how *are* the omens this week?

ASPINALL. You don't want to know about the omens.

CLEMENT. Of course I do. It pays to be informed, doesn't it? We can't bury our heads in the sand.

ASPINALL. You don't *believe* in omens.

CLEMENT. Even so. I like to keep abreast of which black cat has gone under what. Come on, what are the portents?

ASPINALL. Not fantastic.

CLEMENT. No. No, well they wouldn't be, would they. But I can take it.

ASPINALL. Okay. Let's see.

Last Tuesday, in Taston, a butcher cleaved open a pig and found an image of Christ our Lord in the spleen.

On Wednesday, in Long Compton, the water in the well was found turned red and was thought, at first, to have become wine.

In the early hours of Thursday morning, a flotilla of thirty-four toads, riding lily pads like little boats, was seen on the Evenlode, travelling downstream towards Moreton-in-Marsh though, when they reached the county border, they sank below the surface in sick and unified silence.

In the schoolhouse, in Adderbury, the woodworms have got their marching orders. Their exodus took from Friday until Saturday and they left behind beams and cupboard doors which, when knocked, are said to ring like bells with their absence.

And only yesterday, in Spelsbury, a woman was delivered of fourteen rabbits and a cat which, though they had been peaceable in the womb and almost never kicked, began to fight on being born. The rabbits were weaker but they had the advantage of numbers, and the whole affair ended in a stalemate, with terrible injuries on both sides, and the mother could not stop crying.

And last night I watched the moon dip down three times behind the ridge and bob back up like a cork.

ASPINALL *turns back to* CLEMENT.

Yesterday we watched birds pour across the sky from dawn until dusk, right to left – that's the bad direction – and they were blotting out the sun with their bodies. It was twilight at midday. You *saw* it.

Clem, you *saw* it.

CLEMENT. They were just birds.

ASPINALL *turns away.*

And, if we'd been standing somewhere else, they'd have been flying left to right. The *good* direction. We should have just turned round, only I didn't think of it.

What do you want me to say? That the world's ending? Would that be helpful?

ASPINALL. You could stop pretending. Then we could face up to it. /

CLEMENT. Face up to *what*? How do we face up to it? /

ASPINALL. We could at least *talk* about it /

CLEMENT. This is what facing up to it looks like. This is as good as it gets. We ring the bells and we maybe get frazzled, or we don't and we get killed some other way a bit later. And I *want* to talk about it, by the way /

ASPINALL. I don't mean that /

CLEMENT. making a plan, being pragmatic, it's you that won't /

ASPINALL. that's because we've *done* that, I've said *no* to that, that's not what I mean.

CLEMENT. Okay. No, I know.

Lightning. Count two. Thunder.

–

I've been having dreams.

ASPINALL. Yeah. Me too. Last night I dreamed I was a ham.

CLEMENT. Right.

In a good way or a bad way?

ASPINALL. Hard to tell. I wasn't eaten. That's something.

CLEMENT. My dreams are recurring.

They come back – the same ones.

ASPINALL. I know what recurring means.

CLEMENT. Sorry.

ASPINALL. It means coming back, again and again.

CLEMENT. Yeah.

ASPINALL. Dreams of what?

CLEMENT. There's a boat. Like, I'm usually in a boat. Or by a wall.

ASPINALL. Right. Is that what a recurring dream is?

CLEMENT. I'm catching babies – that's the recurring bit.

ASPINALL. Like a midwife.

CLEMENT. No, in my apron. Like someone catching fruit falling from a tree.

ASPINALL. You're wearing an apron?

CLEMENT. I tend to be, in dreams.

Sometimes I'm out in a little boat in the sea – a rough sea, like in books. And they're throwing their babies out to me in the boat, because I guess the shore is a bad place to be. They're throwing them to *me* so I can take them somewhere safe. But I don't know anywhere safe. Or how to look after a baby. Or sail.

And sometimes I'm on one side of a wall, and the babies are coming over. That's worse, that one, because you can't know where they're coming from.

They shouldn't have trusted me.

I wake up, and I feel so awful. I'd have done pretty much anything. But I could never catch all of them.

ASPINALL *makes some kind of sign.*

What are you doing?

ASPINALL. I'm absolving you.

CLEMENT. Oh. Is that all it takes?

ASPINALL. For a *dream*, definitely.

CLEMENT. Okay.

ASPINALL. I mean, who's putting you in charge of that stuff? You're very bad at catching.

CLEMENT. Yeah.

ASPINALL. You know what my mum would say?

CLEMENT. What would she say?

ASPINALL. She'd say it's a good sign. She goes to the almanac. Looks under babies, brackets, catching in the apron like fruit from a tree, turns to page forty-five, says it means everything will go right tonight. Forget all that other stuff. When the storm is overhead we'll ring out the bells and everyone will hear it, and they'll know that we're here looking out for them. And the clouds will part and the lightning will fizzle out, and the fungus will retreat, and the fish will stay in the ponds. The lambs will be born healthy, with one head each. The dreams will stop. And then we'll go home.

CLEMENT. Could be.

ASPINALL. We'll uncover the perfect peal by chance. The perfect two-person peal. The evidence will be irrefutable.

CLEMENT *doesn't react*. ASPINALL *shakes his arm again*.

CLEMENT. What?

ASPINALL. Go on.

CLEMENT. Okay.

(*Wearily.*) We'll ring the bells and the clouds will part, and we'll stand in the churchyard like two Moseses, and gaze up at proof, at last, of a contactable campanologist God and/or a new branch of meteorological science. How's that?

ASPINALL. It's good.

CLEMENT. Yeah.

He turns to ASPINALL *determinedly*.

I think it means – in the dream, I couldn't save all of them, I never could. But I could do *something*. /

ASPINALL. We are doing something. /

CLEMENT. I could catch *you*, I could /

ASPINALL. Last time, Mum knew things would go well.

CLEMENT. Aspinall /

ASPINALL. She'd seen it. Tea leaves.

CLEMENT. You won't listen?

ASPINALL. She knew we'd come home.

CLEMENT. –

And this time?

ASPINALL. She didn't say. I forgot to ask.

There is the faint sounds of bells. CLEMENT *hears it.*

CLEMENT. Listen!

ASPINALL. I *have* listened. Again and again I've listened /

CLEMENT. Not that! Listen – bells.

ASPINALL. Where?

CLEMENT. There.

ASPINALL. Now, who's that? The heart of it must be, what, two miles away?

CLEMENT. Just under. Could be from Chadlington. They have that high bell.

They listen. They hear the high bell. They are suddenly uncontrollably hopeful.

ASPINALL. That's Roscoe!

CLEMENT. And his uncle!

ASPINALL. And three volunteers!

CLEMENT. With his new peal!

ASPINALL. That's Roscoe and his new peal!

CLEMENT *(shouting upwards)*. That'll bring down this bastard!

ASPINALL *(also shouting upwards)*. It's a new science!

They are leaping around, jumping on the benches.

CLEMENT. It's meteorology!

ASPINALL. It's theology!

CLEMENT. It's musicology!

They stop to listen. The bells ring on. There is a flash. After two seconds there is a rumble of thunder and the bells stop. CLEMENT *and* ASPINALL *look at each other.*

–

–

ASPINALL. Could be taking a break. Resting on their laurels, because they know it's worked.

Because they know it's *worked*, Clem.

CLEMENT *cries.* ASPINALL *comforts him.*

Some time passes.

(*Mostly to himself.*) Just fields now. Just fields between them and us.

CLEMENT. When did we see him last?

ASPINALL. I don't know.

CLEMENT. We should know. We need to know.

ASPINALL. Last week? At the common. Yeah, it was when we all went out to the common. I didn't see him after that, did you?

CLEMENT. No.

ASPINALL. We had a fire. We got him laughing – well, you did. I hadn't seen that in a while.

CLEMENT. He gets in his head. He was thinking about the bells.

ASPINALL. But you made him laugh.

CLEMENT. I wasn't mean to him? Sometimes I was mean to him.

ASPINALL. You weren't mean to him.

CLEMENT. I didn't tell him… I didn't tell him it wouldn't work?

ASPINALL. No, you didn't. You made him laugh.

CLEMENT. Because he was trying things. That was good.
I respected that.

ASPINALL. Yeah.

CLEMENT. I love you.

ASPINALL. I know.

CLEMENT. I love you completely.

ASPINALL. Clem, I know.

CLEMENT. Good.

ASPINALL. And I love you.

CLEMENT. I was just making sure it was in there. In case
tonight is…

I can see you running it back in your mind, years on. 'What
was the last thing he said to me? Going on about
mushrooms.'

ASPINALL. It won't be tonight.

CLEMENT. But if it *was*.

ASPINALL. Then it's alright. It's all okay.

A pause. ASPINALL *sits too. They are both thinking,
separately.*

He never taught us how to do the peal. The perfect peal.
Maybe he wrote it down somewhere.

CLEMENT. It doesn't work.

ASPINALL. Don't say that.

CLEMENT. The bells don't *work*, Aspinall. How could they?
How could they stop a storm, or a fire, or a flood? How could
they ring these dreams out?

ASPINALL. Stranger things have happened.

CLEMENT. Have they?

ASPINALL. You know they have. You see stranger things happen every day. Besides, you've seen it work. The bells are rung – the storm ends. And if it doesn't end here, it ends somewhere else. It always ends – it's always ended before.

CLEMENT. That's correlation.

ASPINALL. What?

CLEMENT. It's when /

ASPINALL. I know what it means.

CLEMENT. Storms just end.

ASPINALL. Because of the bells.

CLEMENT. Because they run out of… water, or lightning, or something. That's why they end. They just end. And in the meantime, how many got frazzled?

ASPINALL. You have to try *something*. And what about the other stuff? The mushrooms? The fires?

CLEMENT. They never end. Not properly. I mean, look at this.

CLEMENT *gestures at the mushrooms which have been growing everywhere. There are limbs of ivy growing through the stones. There is moss. Rain begins to drip in.*

If you just go – just go home, and I'll be fine, and I /

ASPINALL. I said I won't.

CLEMENT. Please /

ASPINALL. I can't, Clem. It works best with two. At *least* two, that's what they say. Which makes sense. More sound.

And anyway, we come as a pair. Everyone knows.

He saw her die? Billy?

CLEMENT *nods.*

And what did it get him? An extra three months?

CLEMENT. Five.

ASPINALL. You'd wish that on me?

A moment of tension.

Thinking the conflict has passed, ASPINALL *wanders away from* CLEMENT, *musing to himself.*

If we do go tonight, I'd like to be buried in the field by Tank Farm, under the tree. I've left instructions.

In ideal times, I think I might have liked to get very rich and important, and my tomb would be very... it would be like those ones through there – (*He points to the body of the church.*) with one of these on top.

ASPINALL *lies on a bench on his back with his arms folded over his chest. He sits up to speak.*

And I'd have a sword or something.

Or an axe.

CLEMENT *is not looking at him.* ASPINALL *is trying to get a reaction.*

Or a crossbow.

But I'll settle for just my name, since it's now.

Did you leave instructions?

CLEMENT. Yeah, I wrote something down.

ASPINALL. You told them about the field? The tree?

CLEMENT. Course I did.

ASPINALL. And what about the stone?

CLEMENT. I don't want a stone. Let the corn grow over me.

ASPINALL. How will people know where you are?

CLEMENT. Well, they'll find you and look a little to the left, and there I'll be, just like always.

Besides, we've established. I'll join the mushrooms. I'll go whizzing around underground and pop up in Borneo. Or in

Chadlington. Or I'll scramble through your kitchen floor, say a quick hello. Or I'll come back here. Spend what's left of it in here, with the rest of them.

The mushrooms wriggle their gills, or make some kind of subtle sound.

I wouldn't be lonely, would I? I mean, who's here? If they come back, who's here? Just in the last year, who's here?

ASPINALL. Well, there was Roscoe's dad. His uncle Bart. Linden's cousin with the long hair.

CLEMENT. Your cousin Polly.

ASPINALL. Your uncle Wilbur.

CLEMENT. Lauren's grandmother. And the organist.

ASPINALL. The doctor and the priest. The warden.

CLEMENT. That old man with the sticks.

ASPINALL. That old man with the teeth.

CLEMENT. Dusty and your godmother.

ASPINALL. Old Tony. And Mr Welbourne.

CLEMENT. Jefferson's dad's second wife.

ASPINALL. And his third.

CLEMENT. And Jefferson's dad. And Jefferson.

ASPINALL. And out of our lot – (*Counting on his fingers.*) James, Megan, Jude, Zibby, Mac... Roscoe.

CLEMENT. And the butcher.

ASPINALL. Butchers.

CLEMENT. The one in the fire and – ?

ASPINALL. The one that got sick.

CLEMENT. Oh yeah.

ASPINALL. The odds aren't good out there.

CLEMENT. The odds aren't good in here.

ASPINALL. But I'd *rather* be here. I'd rather it happen here.

What do you want me to do? Go out there on my own? Wait for a flood to sweep me up? Or a fire?

A rumble of thunder.

CLEMENT. What if we both left?

ASPINALL. What?

CLEMENT. What if we just went somewhere right now. Far away.

ASPINALL. Yeah. Imagine it.

Not even… not even ring the bells. Just walk away?

CLEMENT. Yeah.

ASPINALL. We never could.

CLEMENT. I know.

ASPINALL. They're all listening. Out there, in their houses with the wind trying to get under the rooves and lift them off, and the rain trying to break the windows. And the lightning. Maybe they're getting low on hope. But they're waiting to hear the bells.

CLEMENT. I know.

ASPINALL. So we couldn't.

CLEMENT. I didn't mean it, really. I was just dreaming.

ASPINALL. It's okay.

CLEMENT. We couldn't leave your mother.

ASPINALL. Even though she's so…

CLEMENT. You love her.

ASPINALL. Yeah.

CLEMENT. *I* love her.

ASPINALL. Do you?

CLEMENT. Of course I do.

And my dad. He couldn't lose another one.

ASPINALL *nods*.

(*In a lighter tone*.) You'd never get over it – you'd be
a wreck. I'd be fine, my heart's as hard as a stone, but you –
I'd be tending to you, mopping your guilt-stricken brow for
the rest of our lives.

ASPINALL. Yeah, probably.

CLEMENT. We'd hear bells in our sleep.

ASPINALL. No change there, then.

CLEMENT. I was just dreaming.

The point's moot anyway. It's like this everywhere.

ASPINALL. Where would we go?

CLEMENT. If we left?

ASPINALL. If we left.

CLEMENT. Which we wouldn't.

ASPINALL. Which we wouldn't, but *if* we did.

CLEMENT. We always said we'd go and live on a boat. Do you
remember that?

ASPINALL. Course.

CLEMENT. So we'd patch up the boat properly. We'd take it
down the Glyme. Like Noah. Finally get past the point where
the Isis becomes the Thames.

ASPINALL. Things might be easier over there.

CLEMENT. Let's say yes. Let's say we sail east, and we leave
dark clouds behind. No more storms. And we get to the sea.

ASPINALL. Noah took his family.

CLEMENT. Yeah, *some* of them. And he left everyone else behind.

ASPINALL. Do you think he heard them banging on the bottom of the boat?

CLEMENT. I think he did. I think he must have.

It couldn't be us. *You'd* let them all aboard, the boat sinks, animals drowning two by two – there's a reason God didn't pick us, I suppose.

ASPINALL. Things might even out. One of these days. The bad patch ends. And that's when we'll see some more of the world.

Lightning. Count one. Extreme thunder.

CLEMENT *stands, suddenly agitated. He touches the mushroom on his shoulder – he looks upwards.*

CLEMENT. Help me.

The mushrooms react.

There is a sound, like someone knocking at the door. They are both startled.

ASPINALL. What's that?

CLEMENT. I… I don't know.

There could be someone out there.

ASPINALL. It's just the wind. A branch.

CLEMENT. They want to come in.

ASPINALL. Maybe I don't want them here.

CLEMENT. They'll catch their deaths.

ASPINALL. Aren't they safer out there? Isn't that what you think?

CLEMENT. We won't make them ring the bells.

Another knock on the door.

Let them in.

ASPINALL. They can *wait*.

CLEMENT. There's no time.

> *They look at one another.* ASPINALL *knows what* CLEMENT *is going to do.*

> ASPINALL *strides to the door stage-left and opens it. It is wild outside.*

ASPINALL (*shouting into the wind*). Hello?

> Is anyone out there?

> ASPINALL *looks back at* CLEMENT, *who is watching him.*

> ASPINALL *steps out of the door.* CLEMENT *shuts him out, locking the door.*

> CLEMENT *leans his back against the door. There is a hammering from outside, which eventually subsides.*

> *Some time passes.*

> ASPINALL *enters through the other door.*

> CLEMENT *leaps to his feet.*

> ASPINALL *shakes water from his hair.*

CLEMENT. I locked it – the main doors. I came here this morning. I made *sure* they were locked.

ASPINALL. I know. I came here after. I unlocked them. We can all scheme.

CLEMENT. I thought you'd be locked out. And I'd ring the bells. And maybe I'd see you tomorrow.

> I'm sorry.

> CLEMENT *takes a step towards* ASPINALL, *who flinches backwards, as though expecting an attack.* CLEMENT *holds up his hands.*

> That was it, that was my attempt.

> I don't want you to die.

CLEMENT *sits down.* ASPINALL *sits beside him.*

A pause.

ASPINALL. It's filling up in there – (*Pointing to the door to the church.*)

CLEMENT. With what?

CLEMENT *strides to the door and looks in – if we can see through, we see huge mushrooms, maybe other plants.*

ASPINALL. Mushrooms. Mainly. I had to fight my way through.

CLEMENT *goes and looks.*

CLEMENT. Now *this* is a disgrace, isn't it? All this, just while we've been talking. That never used to happen. I admit it. When we were kids. We used to talk for hours, didn't we?

ASPINALL. Yeah.

CLEMENT. And nothing grew while we were talking, did it?

I wanted a life like they had.

ASPINALL. Ordinary?

CLEMENT. Yeah. And long.

ASPINALL. We just came here at a bad time, I suppose.

CLEMENT. Yeah.

CLEMENT *wipes his eyes.*

Ha. These storms! Bring out all this… stuff. Or maybe it's the music. *Every* time.

ASPINALL. What music?

CLEMENT. Don't you hear that?

They listen. Behind the storm, there is organ music playing.

Church music.

ASPINALL. I hear it.

CLEMENT. Who's playing it? No one else should be here.

ASPINALL. Maybe it's the mushrooms.

CLEMENT. Could be. Maybe they've got into the pipes.

ASPINALL. Yeah. Now that I listen, it's not like any of the hymns I know.

CLEMENT. No. It's probably about... spores, or something. Or mulch.

ASPINALL. That's nice, isn't it?

CLEMENT. Is it?

ASPINALL. At least *they're* not worried. They'll keep on singing.

CLEMENT. What'll we do tomorrow?

ASPINALL. I've got some jobs. The usual and then I've got some weeding and I've got to fix that gate.

CLEMENT. We'll go back for those apples. From the witch-house.

ASPINALL. Yeah. And then I think there's going to be a match on the common. They're short of players because... well, for obvious reasons.

CLEMENT. You can play. I'll watch. I'll lie under a tree.

ASPINALL. It'll be wet.

CLEMENT. I'll stand under a tree.

ASPINALL. I'll plant you a tree to stand under.

Pause.

CLEMENT. You know, I think it's brightening up.

They laugh.

They look up – lightning and thunder – close together.

ASPINALL. Ready?

CLEMENT *nods*.

They face each other by the bell ropes.

They grasp the ropes in unison.

CLEMENT. Wait.

Keep your feet together.

ASPINALL. Okay.

They ring the bells.

Darkness.

The bells keep ringing, fading slowly into silence.

End.

A Nick Hern Book

Bellringers first published as a paperback original in Great Britain in 2024 by Nick Hern Books Limited, The Glasshouse, 49a Goldhawk Road, London W12 8QP, in association with Ellie Keel Productions, Atticist and Hampstead Theatre

Bellringers copyright © 2024 Daisy Hall

Daisy Hall has asserted her right to be identified as the author of this work

Cover image: Ciaran Walsh

Designed and typeset by Nick Hern Books, London
Printed in Great Britain by Mimeo Ltd, Huntingdon, Cambridgeshire PE29 6XX

A CIP catalogue record for this book is available from the British Library

ISBN   978 1 83904 379 6

www.nickhernbooks.co.uk/environmental-policy

www.nickhernbooks.co.uk

facebook.com/nickhernbooks

twitter.com/nickhernbooks